# *From Autism*

# *to Beyond*

### *A Mother's Hope*

*Marietta Colston-Davis*

Colston Davis Group
Atlanta, Georgia

ISBN- (trade paperback) 979-8-9857988-0-7

ISBN- (eBook) 979-8-9857988-1-4

First Edition: February 2022
Publisher- Colston Davis Group
Alpharetta, GA 30022

Cover design- JL Woodson
of Woodson Creative Studio www.woodsoncreativestudio.com
Publishing Consultant- Naleighna Kai www.naleighnakai.com
Editor- MarZé Scott www.marzescott.com
Beta reader- Marie McKenzie www.marielmckenzie.com
Beta reader- Christine Pauls www.christinepauls.com

# From Autism
# to Beyond

*A Mother's Hope*

Marietta Colston-Davis

# ♦ ACKNOWLEDGEMENTS ♦

I want to thank Sara Cole and Frances Colston for being amazing contributors to this book, and more importantly the wind beneath my wings. You've both been here from the beginning and believed in me when I didn't believe in myself. You are my two amazing sorority sisters and I love you both. The story simply could not have been told without you.

To Lakeisha Johnson, who I met as you taught Sunday School to special needs children at Victory World Church. You told me I had a story. Thank you.

To Marva Hicks, forty plus years of friendship and you have made every bit of this lifetime worthwhile. Your love for me and Tyler has been nothing less than relentless. I'm grateful for you every day.

*Marietta Colston-Davis*

# Chapter 1

## A LITTLE BIT ABOUT ME

Understanding this journey is to know a little bit about me. Have you ever heard of Urbandale, Iowa? No? I'm sure many people haven't unless they grew up there. The only family of color, let me rephrase, the only Black family to reside in the town with the first black child to attend the school district from preschool until graduation. My older sister and I didn't attended the same school, and she was a few grades ahead of me. With that detail being revealed, this almost goes without saying—I've always been keenly aware of differences.

From as far back as I can remember, there were constant reminders that let the world know that something about me was different. The hue of my complexion in an all-White town wasn't enough. Being smarter than the average pre-school aged student wasn't even a cherry on top. It could've been that I was too observant for a child. As a consequence, I worked harder, felt more insecure, and expected all aspects and elements of my life to be perfect. For example, my first-grade teacher,

Mrs. Hughes, said to my mother that she wasn't sure *how* to teach me as she had never taught a *Negro* child before. At the time, I was only four years old (yes, I was pretty sharp) and I had questions. With a degree of certainty, I'm sure Mrs. Hughes had her own reservations considering both of my parents were college educated and had been since the early 1950's, something that wasn't as common as it is today.

Late one evening, I overheard my parents talking about me and my sister and remember feeling cursed for being different. I'm sure that they weren't saying anything inherently bad, however I was uncomfortable being the topic of discussion. One wouldn't think that a child would know what it is to feel like she's an outsider, but then if a person constantly exists in an environment where she (or he) is the only one who looks like she does, thinks like she does, or speaks like she does, it's learned early on that being unique is a problem. Being unlike others can be traumatizing, especially for children, as a wayward thought or disagreement can have lasting effects on young, impressionable minds. My parents helped me to understand that my differences were not only a privilege, but also a gift.

I knew that I'd create a picture-perfect life for my child. I never wanted them to feel like they were a burden or that being different was a bad thing. I played the future like a movie in my mind over and over again—where I'd live, what my husband would do, and how adorable my children would be. They would go on to be the most successful people in the Peyton Place town of the Imaginaryville of my mind. I look back on that now and realize many of these thoughts and feelings stemmed from the way "different" was unconsciously defined; it screamed imperfection for me and my older sister. As a result, perfection came to be my standard.

My sister, Rhonda, was six years older than me. She was the first experience and impact that I had with a person who lived with special needs. The extent of her disabilities was never explained to me. One detail was all I knew; she was born with the umbilical cord around her neck which caused a lack of oxygen to her brain.

Rhonda appeared to be like most big sisters, however I was about seven years old when I realized her distinctions. Simply put, she was a bit "slower" than me. She attended a school outside of our neighborhood and required a bit of extra work from our parents. I had an inkling of what that meant as I was advanced for my age. If my sister was older and "slower", then I had to be a freak of nature.

My mother, a very spiritual woman, was the most patient. "God made each you differently and He loves all his creations. She's your sister and you are family," she said. That was the declaration. It made sense to my young intellect but didn't seem like enough of an explanation. I accepted what my mother said and limited my inquiries—once the answer is understood to be what it is, the need to ask for any more information is laid to rest. At any rate, we lived our lives, along with our dog, Prince, and my parents. Our family was idyllic to be candid. Growing up, like most little sisters, I looked up to Rhonda. She was *my* big sister and friend until the differences continued to separate us.

Distance is a funny thing—physically it can make a heart grow fonder, however, emotionally it's heartbreaking. Rhonda and I grew apart. Was it our ages or our differences? In some regard it didn't much matter as the distance between us swelled. My peers would ask "What's wrong with your sister?" or "Why isn't she like you?" Should a twelve-year-old *have* to explain why her sibling is not like her or another? Doesn't seem fair, but by the time I had to retell the story given to me, or discern how even relatives compared us, what I knew was I had to protect her. I defended her ferociously against the bullies who were more inclined to tease her than to befriend her. They never had to understand her limitations, nor could they find a space to be kind. I loved and accepted her as a gift from God.

I doubled down on my dream of perfection for my future children and believed, in my own odd way, that would make the world alright.

And then autism happened. I mean, imagine the heartbreak as the picture-perfect village I dreamt of over the years was dismantled by the hands of adults and peers alike, and then the professionals. No explanations, only theories. Research offered no answers. Autism happens and no one knows exactly why or how. It presents itself and all of its differences and challenges, a condition that occurs with no blame to give. The "curse" felt like it increased three-fold—my weeping was louder, my overeating became more extreme, my defensiveness was more amplified, and at times, my disconnection from emotion grew deeper. But then, my determination was greater; my work ethic grew stronger; and *my* demands of all the people that impacted my son were monumental.

This is a story of many emotions, but three above all.

They are faith, hope and love. 1 Corinthians 13. For me, the greatest of these has been love.

# Chapter Two

## FIRST SIGNS OF TROUBLE

My world tilted on its axis the moment my son spoke his first words at five years old— "Mama, hungry."

Yes, I said his first words, that I could clearly understand, spoken from the backseat of the car, were unusual but nonetheless emotional for a mother who was scared of what the doctors said his life would be like.

In the joy of childbirth, a mother will see all of his or her beauty and can overlook or not recognize what isn't considered normal. My son had doe brown eyes, a button nose, ten fingers and ten toes—he was perfect.

Tyler was about a week old when I noticed something and became concerned; maybe a better word would be alarmed—he didn't make eye contact with me when he breastfed. As a new mother, you gaze into your baby's eyes, communicating without word that you are connected at a soul level and only the two of you understand. I contemplated where his young thoughts might be as my admiration and joy turned to worry as

I observed his behavior. Taking mental notes, I began to compile a list of my concerns. Feedings became tense as they turned into a time for inspecting his responses, or lack thereof, to my desire to bond with him.

The realization that your child seems different than other babies is something that every mother fears at one point or another. Other babies smiled at their mothers, crawled like speed racer, and gazed upon their parents as if they were the only faces in the world that mattered. Though a mother doesn't do it on purpose, she may compare her child's skills and abilities to other children, to what appears to be normal for everyone else. I did. The differences, major or minor, were kept in the recesses of my mind.

As mothers, we're inclined to think we'll move past what isn't obvious and hope for the best. Deep inside, we often wonder. Play groups, which were supposed to offer some kind of solace and support, only brought about anxiety and exhaustion. Nervous mothers are constantly bombarded by updates from every other mother in the peer group about what accomplishments their own little bundles of joy have performed. Bobby smiled at his mother. Jenny chattered using new words—it was hard to not get jealous of even the babies who are doing the 'normal' and 'natural' things. I suspect it's the same way couples feel if they struggle to conceive and friends or family members announce a pregnancy that breezes by for nine months without a single complication, producing a healthy, happy, bouncing baby. Add the advent of social media and heartache seemed to loom around every corner.

Every trip to the pediatrician with Tyler was traumatic. Though I was married, my son and I were the only ones at these appointments, which put me on edge from the get-go. It fell to me to report every single nuance of his nutrition, sleep patterns, and behavior. One word could almost accurately describe being the lone recipient of the overwhelming amounts of information that the doctors and other medical professionals shared with me—drowning. Some of it was scary, while more of it was baffling, and I could only rely on my own strength and faith to get through it.

As a mother, I'd encourage any other parent to trust their gut instincts and the certainty that God places on their hearts, no matter how frightening or challenging a situation might seem. The doctors, often in an effort to prepare you for the journey ahead, offer the worst-case scenarios, all of the what-he-or-she-will-never-be-able-to-do stories. What these physicians didn't understand was that a lot of what they said was taken with a grain of salt as I believed that God always had the final say.

The term "mother's instinct" isn't just a made-up, but a real, scientific thing that is found in the brains of all mammals. Mothers have an innate knowledge of things that their babies need and when situations are not quite right. The sooner one can come to grips with a less-than-optimal situation, the better the response to it. As I look back over my life, I think about the many times that inner voice was telling me to check on something or that I wasn't just imagining things. Had I listened to that voice, I would've avoided several pitfalls in my life. I knew one thing if I knew nothing else—my son couldn't be the victim of even one poor choice. Tyler was destined to be a guiding light, a beacon of hope, and an example to those who said he wouldn't and couldn't win in life.

Isolated. Alone. Desperate. Did I mention *alone*? When I arrived at our sprawling two story home, I shared the prognosis with my husband, Tyler's father, and it wasn't received well. Whether he didn't want to believe it, or the weight was too much to handle for a man's firstborn son, I don't quite know. What I did understand as he walked out of the room, away from me and Tyler, was that I'd have to shoulder the responsibility of our son's well-being from that moment forward. I'm so grateful for the strength and support of my parents and my sorority sisters during that time. They kept me encouraged, telling me to push forward in my quest for answers. Most of all, I thank God for being an ever-present source of love and light.

From dusk until dawn was the most difficult period for me after Tyler's initial diagnosis. To say that I was ready for bedtime is a gross understatement. I needed to take off the mask. I could stop being the corporate mogul, the sorority sister, the perfect daughter, and the wife who hid her husband's addictions. It was the time that I looked in the mirror and felt no black girl magic; only the pain of a woman who had been broken for many years and all the circumstances and events that caused the damage that was concealed by a superior work ethic. Just me. My cigarettes, at times vodka, other occasions Oreos and Doritos became my not-so-guilty pleasures—they comforted me when nothing else would.

An hour can feel like a lifetime when you're unclear where you're going. What was I supposed to do? Debilitated by the closing walls of this thing called Autism, by addiction, responsibility, and the need to never let my parents down, and now Tyler's future was left in my hands. There's pressure in always seeing the glass as half full, which for the most part it was. However, by the end of the day, that glass was empty and the next day was fast-approaching whether or not I had anytime to fill it to even halfway again.

I never was quite sure if Tyler understood that he was different from other children, or that he knew his mama was crazy, but he knew something. Though he didn't speak, it was something in his facial expressions—the eyes convey a myriad of emotions. When I'd be at my lowest moments, expecting the worst and hoping for the best, each morning Tyler would shock me. He'd be watching the door from his crib when I'd peer into his room. He seemed to know when I had been up all night long crying, eating, or both—how could I explain the defeat I felt to anyone? To *my* child? Slowly and almost by accident, I became robotic. The one thing I could control was my work. I focused on "making the donuts"—that part of my life came with more ease than other parts. Losing wasn't a part of my fabric or vocabulary, so I had to put forth effort to stay above water for my son.

Tyler was two and still not speaking and had limited eye contact—I was keenly aware there was an issue. A mother just knows. I had heard of this condition called PDD or Pervasive Developmental Disorder. PDD is a catch-all phrase for issues that sit on the Autism Spectrum. This umbrella term was what I needed to start researching symptoms for this disorder as I prepared myself for the uncertain road ahead.

From an early age, I was convinced that Tyler struggled with something on the spectrum even though none of the doctors had said the same. They always wanted to wait for milestones and markers, and they thought I was supposed to watch and wait with them. I was expected to stand idly by, anticipating for the calendar to move. Time was of the essence, so that wasn't an option for me. If there's any advice I can offer to another parent who recognizes that their child is struggling it would be to be proactive. Do as much research as you can and get an even footing with the professionals when it comes to knowledge. It's a tall task, but necessary. There's so much that physicians have learned about spectrum disorders and yet so much they're still learning. One would be surprised how few experts you'll find in the medical field when it comes to autism. The average pediatrician has to have a breadth of knowledge of growth and development, but not necessarily a depth. They are focused on the bigger warning signs of things like malnutrition, developmental milestones, and struggles with feeding. Autism is already a murky subject for most doctors who are not specialists, and in my experience they were inclined to keep delaying the prognosis. However, if you're persistent and steadfast with your concerns, a specialist will be brought into the mix. It's exhausting, but worth the energy—don't give up.

I recall one morning peering into Tyler's room, thinking how patient he was for a little one. For the most part, I'd hear him moving about in his crib, but he didn't cry loud when it was morning, almost like he understood the emotions that challenged me. More than I care to admit, my daily routine often started with wiping any tears off my face. His father was most likely not home, and if he were, he'd be lounging in the living room recliner, high from an all-night binge or passed out asleep.

One particular morning, I said, "Hey T-Money. How's Mommies baby boy?" Tyler's bright, big, beautiful eyes met me as he stood in his crib with a huge smile on his face. He grabbed my face, little hands on each cheek and pulled me close. He examined me as if he had a window into my soul as he gazed at me. He rubbed my cheek as to wipe the places my tears had fallen, gave me a kiss, then patted my head or arm,

I don't recall now. I was freaked out, to say the least. This is a big deal because autism is a disorder that lacks emotional connection and eye contact. With that being said, it could've been my imagination, but I'll take it for what it was—comfort, his way of saying we were going to be alright.

I broke out into laughter, we both giggled, and he was the most cooperative he had ever been. It was a breakthrough moment, and I believe he knew I needed help. This is how I remember our journey starting—a child that worked relentlessly to please, deliver, and exceed.

Attending the birthday party of my goddaughter with Tyler provided an eye-opening revelation. At that birthday party, children were everywhere. Some were related, others had never met each other before. Every single one of them was completely capable of interacting with each other. Tyler cried and cried for hours. He wouldn't be touched or make eye contact.

Tyler's father stayed home that day. He was knee-deep in the addiction that was tearing our already fragile family apart. Early on, he seldom wanted to see Tyler around other kids. Maybe his habits let him stay in the dark about what was going on. Out of sight, out of mind, right? Being alone and having to watch Tyler's every movement was exhausting and scary. Unfortunately, it was par for the course. The pursuit to find help for Tyler was a one-person show ninety-nine percent of the time. I often wonder how I made it through. My mother helped, and his godmother assisted, but it's not the same as having a supportive spouse, the person who shares the same DNA as your child. However, his assistance was too much to ask. The person who had promised to honor me and bring up our child in the way he should go, had completely checked out on both of us.

That party solidified everything I'd been thinking and feeling. Honestly, I didn't deserve to bear the pain of that moment, but I absolutely needed to have it. Tyler was placed against a backdrop of a healthy mix of ages - some older, some younger, some right on his level, but all of them acting well within what the average person would deem the normal range of age-appropriate behaviors. It was hard to not compare him to one or two other children, but the feeling that he was falling behind was more than a notion to swallow.

One thing was certain … it was time to go beyond the pediatrician and get some answers for my son.

*Chapter 3*

## THE DIAGNOSIS - A FEELING CONFIRMED

*Under no circumstances will I allow society to speak to me about my son, I'll be damned if that happens.*

You hear about God putting people in your path so that they can help you along your way. Tyler and I both experienced that early on in the form of his godmother, who is a speech-language pathologist at the University of Illinois.

Some people confuse what a speech-language pathologist does with the services provided by a speech therapist. The latter works with children on pronouncing their sounds right. The former goes deeper into the parts of a child's speech, including things like taking social cues, word choices, receptive vs. expressive dialogue, and correcting physical deficiencies in how sounds are formed.

Thank God Almighty that he blessed us with Tyler's godmother, Sara. After a lengthy discussion with her about his behavior, we felt it would be best to undergo a cross-category evaluation to understand what was going on from a clinical point of view. As you may have figured, a cross-category evaluation is a battery of tests that assess a child's disabilities to measure what services will bring about success in managing behaviors. Sara observed Tyler closely and suspected that there was something happening beneath the surface. She faced her own unique set of challenges as she balanced the conflicting roles of being a professional expert, my dear friend, and Tyler's godmother. To read her thoughts about Tyler's condition, her marvelous take on his life, and the process of discovery, check chapter six.

An assessment sounded like the smartest way forward to me. I wanted answers, no matter what they might be. Any truth would be better than the stomach-churning, head-pounding uncertainty of not knowing. At least, that's what I thought at the time. Little did I know that investigation gave birth to many tests, highs, lows, and spirals.

The morning of the examination, I trusted Tyler would be well rested. I dressed him in soft fleece pants and a t-shirt—it was comfortable for him, and he was adorable. My hands trembled; my nerves quivered up through my arms and up my spine, getting the best of me and my thoughts as I hoped he would respond well to an unfamiliar environment and to people who were alien to him.

We arrived in the near west side area after a long ride from Bolingbrook, a Chicago suburb. I prayed that the waiting room part of the adventure wouldn't be long—Tyler didn't do well waiting and it was paramount for him to put his best foot forward. His father was with me, which should've given me reason to be calm. Instead, it created an added layer of anxiety, but I was elated to finally have his support. He grew to be more involved in Tyler's journey later on.

Time ticked away, and the walls of the waiting room felt like they were shrinking minute by minute. We were called to follow the staff member to a room and asked to answer what felt like a million questions. The cross-category team requested to take Tyler to a different room so they could observe him. The doctors led him out, and I got the sensation like a knife was being twisted in my stomach. Grasping that they were going to scrutinize my son's every move made me ill. Understanding that I couldn't be there to protect him, shattered my confidence as his mother, however this was all a part of the assessment process.

White coats scribbling on clipboards, asking question after question: "Does he play well with other children?" "Does he connect or bond with you?" "What are his favorite activities?" While I answered to the best of my knowledge and observations, my thoughts stayed on and with Tyler.

Then came the point of the interview when we were finally able to observe him via a two-way mirror. As his mother, it was apparent to me that they were seeking something he simply couldn't provide in the form of a response. I wanted my instincts to be wrong, but as time moved along and the testing extended, I knew the outlook wasn't as bright as I once hoped. Maybe, just maybe, my "gut" was wrong. To this day, no one could convince me that the whole day hadn't passed. Even though it was probably only three or four hours, it was an eternity in my mind.

Once the session wrapped up, Tyler's father and I anxiously awaited the results, praying they'd come back quickly. What made matters infinitely worse, at least for me, was that since Sara had been part of Tyler's observation, she held the answers I desperately needed and couldn't speak on her own thoughts until the cross-team had completed their review. We discussed the aspects of the study several times before committing to that series of tests and that facility. Ultimately, we decided since she'd been by my side throughout the process, it made sense for her to continue on the journey with us. Her compassion and patience helped to ease us into the next phase of this trek. This disorder is not "personal"—autism hits families who are economically well-off or impoverished; it affects parents who are highly educated and those who barely graduated high school. In those famous words … *it is what it is*, and now we potentially had to figure out what life was going to look like for Tyler, and how that picture would be drawn by his father and me. We were in a good financial position to ensure that our son got the help he needed to be successful in his life.

The day finally came when Tyler's father and I made the drive back to Chicago from the suburbs. The ride was quiet as neither of us felt like faking the small talk when we both knew that we were preparing for news that would shape our son's existence forever.

The combination of a long, quiet drive and the worry for Tyler's future took its toll before we arrived at the University of Illinois campus. Once again, we were shown into a room with artificial lights, and a sterile hospital smell that made me feel sleepy even though it hadn't been a few hours since I woke up.

The small conference room was dominated by a long table, in each seat along two sides sat the medical practitioners who had examined Tyler. A physical therapist, an occupational therapist, a clinical psychologist, a speech pathologist, and the team lead. Seeing them all in one place struck a chord of fear in me. Their faces were stoic, even ominous, as if they were waiting to drop the biggest of bombs into my life. I knew in my soul the news was going to be confirmation of what I had expected early on instead of what I had hoped and prayed for.

Each physician took time to read what appeared to be reams of paper that comprised of their notes. One doctor broke the thick silence that filled the room, and one by one they explained their findings in what I could only define as "clinical speak". My head throbbed and heat radiated around my face as every doctor in the room talked to us about our son as if we were contemporaries in their field, doing little to translate the cold, medical jargon that was as much a foreign language as Russian or Chinese.

As though they read the confusion in my mind, one staff member summed up all of the pathological lingo into verbiage I could understand, and word that I'd been dreading: "We believe Tyler is autistic or at least on the spectrum. He presents with the following symptoms…"

Honestly, I can't remember what was said after that. It was just too much for me. My chest tightened as breathing became difficult. My husband tried to comfort me. I couldn't speak. Couldn't see. Denial started to set in even before a myriad of questions hit at once:

*How could this be?*

*Why didn't the doctors catch this earlier?*

*Did I do something wrong while I was pregnant?*

*What the hell is really happening here?*

"What does this mean?" I asked passed the lump in my throat once I found my voice. Tears fell relentlessly as my heart ached. I promise you, no matter what I suspected, I wasn't prepared for the confirmation of my fears.

As I gathered my thoughts, and formed my lips around that first question, more inquiries poured out like a raging river:

*"What will school be like for him?"*

*"Will he learn to speak?"*

*"What will his future hold?"*

*"What? What? What?"*

Vague memories are still with me of one of them saying that since he is not verbal, we are not sure what his future will be, but we are confident he will contribute to society in some meaningful way.

My mind stuck on *that* particular statement, fixated on my son growing up to work entry level jobs. That isn't necessarily bad, but his father and I each hold multiple degrees, and we thought—no, we dreamed of our son following in our footsteps. We couldn't conceive the sort of life the doctors alluded to. *Contribute in some meaningful way.* In that moment, something spoke to me, and in hindsight I know that it was the voice of God speaking directly to me. The voice said, "It's done ... go to work." In that instant, I inhaled a deep, cleansing breath, and remembered who *I* was, how amazing my son was, and how powerful my God was.

"Okay. So, what's next?" I asked, searching the faces of the professionals who sat at the table. "What do we do to give my son the best opportunity at life?"

The decision was made—I'd speak life over Tyler and what his possibilities were; I wouldn't talk about his disabilities or what they appeared to be. My faith filled my lungs like fresh air and allowed me to breathe, giving me permission to consider Tyler's life without fear. I knew God was with me and my family. All the uncertainties about my son vanished, and my Fresh Prince of Bel Air, as he later called himself, was born.

# Chapter 4

## THE EMOTIONAL ROLLERCOASTER

The visceral pain can never be described. An empty cry with no voice. A bitterness that is not able to be put into words and the question that echoed in my mind: How do I go on?

No two parents will have the same reaction to learning that their child has autism. For me, devastating pain flared when I heard my son was "not normal", that he might never speak, that my son "would never become the hopes and dreams I had prayed for". With each ounce of courage and strength sustaining me, I still couldn't fathom what seemed to be unreal.

The weeks and months following the diagnosis, I felt in a haze or simply paralyzed—mentally and physically. I was overwhelmed with thoughts of what I might have done wrong. This is fairly common for any mother who has a child with developmental delays or other condition diagnosed in childhood. We can't blame the child. We place the burden on ourselves because it's all that makes sense, but also adds to the weight of our guilt and shame. You start to ask yourself questions like: *Did I take all my prenatal vitamins? Did I get enough folic acid? Enough rest? Should I have taken my maternity leave sooner? Was it my inability to manage my stress from the anxiety of my husband's poor choices and behaviors that caused this trauma while I carried Tyler?*

At that time, early studies indicated it was the mother's lack of connection or distance that impacted the child. This made me fixate on what part I played and how. Maybe this or that had happened or didn't. In an effort to avoid the same issues with my next child, every pamphlet, document, and sheet of paper I could read became like textbooks on the causes of autism. I became a voracious reader and somewhat of an expert in the field. Studying leaflets and attending seminars, I gobbled up new trainings and reviews like a child with Halloween candy. There might not have been a cure, but I was determined to read every shred of evidence I could on what advancements were being made, what trial drugs were being tested, and what techniques were showing progress. These actions gave me some sense of control over the situation. I wasn't blindly clutching at straws anymore, trying to figure out how to help my son and shaking my fist at the great unknown of what could be wrong with him. Instead, I used my acquired knowledge to empower him more and more as well as myself.

Of course, all of those strong moments had their corresponding weak ones. Any time a choice has to be made, I struggled time and again, fighting to hold myself together. I had choices to make—wallow in self-pity, and fall apart, or find a way to dig down deep and rebound to help my child succeed against these very long odds that had been pitted against us. Internal meltdowns became an unhealthy, commonplace emotion. In order for me to gain any amount of solace and control, I learned to fake the funk. "Fake it 'til you make it" was my mantra so that I could make consistent and solid efforts to do whatever it took to help my child. That doesn't mean I wasn't still plagued by doubt, fear, or worry. Many nights the tears flowed as I ate packs of Oreos or bags of Doritos, but I convinced myself to succumb to self-pity wouldn't be in

Tyler's best interest. Forward movement was the only direction I'd take.

Then my world shifted in ways I hadn't expected. What hurt most was the way the world around me treated my son. Friends who had more knowledge than I did and were trained in psychology acted as if they didn't understand anything about autism and I know they knew better.

I tried to make sure Tyler had some amount of "normal" engagement with people other than family. Simple acts broke my heart more often than I had expected. For example, while at a birthday party I overheard someone tell him that he couldn't get a certain color balloon because the birthday girl wanted it and it was *her* birthday. Tyler didn't understand. Tears welled up in his eyes and rolled down his cheeks. Then he let out a heartbreaking howl that didn't stop and couldn't be silenced. I tried to console him, which was always overwhelming. This person didn't know Tyler and couldn't have known the most basic factors in dealing with children who live with autism. He unwittingly unraveled my tightly wound child and then dismissed him like he was an ant under a shoe, and I took it personally. Though I believe it wasn't intentional, that moment of hurt will shadow me to my grave. Often, the behavior of others is more hurtful for the parents and guardians of children on the spectrum as some children with autism don't have a keen awareness of what can be offensive. Sometimes, I still harbor emotions brought on by pure ignorance and other not-so-well-meaning people, but my belief in God has helped me to move past the pettiness a lot of people display.

Mothers need to understand and be prepared for the unexpected, from family members, friends and even professionals. The absolute ignorance and cruelty happens and the foul things you will hear from "normal" people will make you question who needs more serious help—them or my son? Once, someone told me that the Devil was the reason Tyler had autism and made a huge stink about the way he was acting. It's strange and unnerving to think how people of faith would actually accuse God cursing a child, going as far as to ridicule who He made my son to be. Christians, in particular, are often the first to say a child's disability is a curse. Thank God I don't share that thinking. Many times, people would turn up their noses in disgust when Tyler would act out. It isn't unusual for toddlers and preschool aged children to misbehave, but children who live with autism have a rough time self-soothing and self-regulating—their outbursts can be more dramatic than other children's. However, these reactions devastated me and made me want to gather up my son and shield him from the rest of the world. He was so precious, and kind, and didn't deserve that type of treatment. No one does.

One of the most amazing changes in this story for me was the growth I witnessed from my husband. From being disconnected and unsupportive in Tyler's early years to being one of his biggest advocates later in his childhood. He wasn't ashamed of who his son was, even during the times when all I wanted to do was to shelter him. My relationship with him wasn't always the best and the challenges of caring for a child with special needs took a toll on our marriage. In retrospect, I believe our united efforts to ensure the best future for Tyler was the glue that kept us together for more than twenty-four years. Coupled with his addictions and issues, the stresses and struggle could've ended the marriage at a time when Tyler needed us both so desperately, but I'm glad to say that wasn't the case.

Tyler's father defended him against other people when it mattered most. I hope at some point in the future we'll come to reconcile the difficulties between us and celebrate what we accomplished. It can be difficult for men to be fathers of special needs children, especially their sons. They don't know how to react or communicate with them and resulting in turning a blind eye to the problems. Just like my husband wouldn't join me going to a lot of Tyler's pediatric appointments, other fathers would choose to live in the dark in other ways. They try to convince themselves that a little hard work, some roughhousing, watching some sports, going hunting, fishing, or camping will make their sons behave like any of their friend's children. There isn't an invisible "switch" that could change his condition, and I'm not sure that I'd flip it even if there were.

Our second son was born underweight and deaf and once again my self-doubt crept in. I'm not sure how it felt for my husband to have two sons with special needs, or what he endured mentally. He wasn't as open with me about his thoughts, but I know he loves his boys, and they love him. No one could've prepared us for the destruction, devastation, and impact these new developments would have on our marriage and our relationship. Yet, we stood on hope and the spectacular beauty the finish line provided.

# Chapter 5

THE EDUCATIONAL JOURNEY

Once the diagnosis was made, then what? How do we take a two-year-old non-verbal child and prepare him for a future that clearly is unknown? 1 Thessalonians 5:17 demands that we pray without ceasing and this was my petition:

*"As each day begins and ends, I ask God to cover me and help provide me the strength and knowledge to make the proper decisions."*

The term "early intervention" was justifiably demanded, and the numerous medical professionals informed us that we needed to get Tyler in a program that would support his potential future. Early Intervention is the term used to describe the resources that are available to babies and young children with developmental delays and disabilities as well as to their families. These services may include, but aren't limited to a combinations of speech therapy, physical therapy, and occupational therapy, along with types of amenities that are based on the needs of the child and family. Intervening early can also have a significant impact on a child's ability to learn new skills, overcome challenges, and increase success in school and life. Programs, some of them publicly funded, are available in every state and often can be found for free or at reduced cost, to any eligible child.

Armed with this information, the quest began. First, I kept the extensive diagnosis and study completed at the University of Illinois. Little did I know at the time, but the initial report would place me in a category of "informed" parents so that the focus could be more on Tyler's individual educational plan (IEP). We started him on a complete regiment—co-treat therapeutic plan, one that initially worked to regulate him. This program consisted of using weighted vests and therapeutic swings and slides, as well as a speech therapist and an occupational therapist because they involved similar therapy approaches. Both work with clients who have problems with feeding, swallowing, cognitive, posture, and language learning difficulties. It's proven that different approaches to similar issues in a combined session along with a classroom-based early intervention program can help increase outcomes for the child.

So, I took my two-and-a-half-year-old precious, big-eyed beautiful little boy and put him on a school bus to the program at the educational institute in my local school district. Transportation would also pick him up in the afternoon three times a week to take him to private occupational and speech therapists. All of it was a costly and draining endeavor. At the time Tyler was diagnosed, the plethora of resources and tools available now, simply were not in abundance. Much of this therapy was paid for out of pocket. Initially, the costs were astronomical. As the saying goes: to those who much is given, much is required. As time went on, it would require me to learn, investigate, and utilize all the advantages that the state I lived in would offer based upon eligibility.

By the time Tyler had turned three, he greatly improved and advanced beyond a sippy cup which meant overcoming a fear of swallowing to at least trying a few new foods. Reflecting on those times are hilarious as I think about how much he eats today and the fact he will eat anything I cook. Back then, his diet consisted of chicken nuggets and fries. His dad went to remarkable lengths to get him to eat food in "bite-sized" amounts, almost like a little bird feeding their young.

As we progressed through treatment, there were seminars about experimental drugs—yes, we tried a few—with no visible outcome aside from torture on Tyler. He hated needles. I attended every seminar where the great Dr. Temple Grandin was a guest speaker. Fireworks went off in my mind. She was a successful example of someone living with autism, and gave me a newfound hope for Tyler. Her life's work had been to understand her own autistic mind, and to share that knowledge with the world. Her discoveries about autism spectrum disorder have aided in the treatment of individuals with the similar condition. Her appreciation of the human mind facilitated her work with animal behavior and also made her one of the most respected experts in both autism and animal behavior in the world. I found myself most riveted as she expressed how the outside world/stimuli felt to her. Her experience helped me feel more connected to Tyler, and more fully comprehend what the therapists meant when they said, "he thinks in file cabinets", meaning when he needs to retrieve something he goes there to get it. We think in abstract, and he thinks more literally.

So much came together in those early years. I gained knowledge of the condition, the behaviors, the interventions, and the results of our efforts. I knew what services Tyler was entitled to and I carried a folder with all of that information to prepare for meetings with his teachers to amend his education plan at any moment. One thing was certain—every single school district knew when this Mama Bear graced the halls, not only was I informed and educated, but I was also aware of my rights. If things appeared less than optimal for Tyler, I wouldn't hesitate to speak about due process and hire the proper advocate. Now, there are many more resources on the Internet that weren't available before. Every parent should research and take advantage of all the data, make wise decisions, and stay informed.

Give yourself permission to see what appears to be "natural" development for your own child without comparing him or her to others. Autism is a sort of gift that is best understood when you're patient with it. Learning to redefine success and jubilation is what allowed me to embrace each of Tyler's individualized education plans (IEPs) and discuss with teachers as they told me what an amazing job we had done with him. It allowed me to *see* that I was doing right as a parent, and led to our own special kind of celebrations to rejoice in those victories

All in all, phenomenal educators, who were passionate about children with special needs, were so supportive of my son along his journey. As he got older and I became more comfortable with what he needed year to year, we worked with all of the programs and treatments that placed him on a phenomenal path for success as you will read about later in the book.

One final piece of advice for parents embarking on this journey: start early, be persistent, seek to understand before being understood and work with your private therapy team as well as your school district educators to learn about the various treatments that make sense. Everything will work out for you and your child.

# *Chapter 6*

## EXPLORING TYLER'S GIFTS

*A silver lining occurs when you least expect it.*

For all of the worries and concerns I had from Tyler's earliest days about things—his lack of eye contact and disinterest in other children, it was equally obvious that he also had some extraordinary gifts that other children didn't.

As I mentioned in the opening chapter, he stood and walked at the age of nine months. I'm not just talking about pulling up and cruising! He did it all without even the slightest hint of a wobble. That balance was Olympic star quality. He also did things that most young children wouldn't even have a clue of starting—more complicated puzzles and solving a Rubik's cube. It became clear to me that there was more to him than we could've ever imagined, but we didn't know what to make of any of this. Somehow, the ashes of the disability were traded for the beauty of incredible capabilities.

## TYLER—MY WONDER KID

Children, by nature, are explorers and Tyler absolutely was no different in that manner. At a young age, he put his fingers to a keyboard and started playing but did so with no formal training. Again, this wasn't just any child coming across the instrument and pressing the keys over and over because he liked the way it sounded. This was a boy picking up patterns way before he had any formal training or examples of how making music was done. He could play a song after hearing it a few times. I'm sure I'd have a hard time accomplishing that fete even if I had listened to a song all day.

Tyler continued to amaze me with his ingenuity. He *knew* how to create from what I can only believe was from what he imagined or heard in his mind without the influence of any external instruction. One of his teachers used the term 'savant' to describe what he did. That term gets thrown around a lot when kids show great abilities at a young age. An autistic savant is *someone with autism who also has a single extraordinary area of knowledge or ability.* Could this be what they mean by savant? How is it possible for my child not to speak, yet play the keyboard, solve a Rubik's cube, or navigate to any Burger King in Ann Arbor Michigan. To this day, I'm not sure if Tyler is, or is not, an autistic savant, but there are interesting facets of his life that demonstrate rare skills.

He had other gifts that were slow to develop, but when they did, it was like watching the sun burst from behind the clouds and light up the entire sky. Over time, Tyler learned to embrace the world around him and love it just as much. He was ten, maybe twelve years old when his personality formed, and he enjoyed the festivities of big holidays like Halloween and Christmas. From a quiet little boy who didn't even want to look at his own mother to a happy kid reveling in candy and presents, the transformation was remarkable for all of us. He was, and still is, incredibly handsome, so he enjoys attention everywhere he goes. He has learned to embrace my love of shopping as well.

Tyler loved keeping his room clean and helping me tidy the kitchen. One gift of autism that many children share is the power of organizing, and he is no exception. While we were worried and scared when we first received that diagnosis, it became clear over time that the early intervention was the best thing that could've happened for us. Moving in that wisdom, it allowed us to work on his connectedness to the world around him, to pump up his love of sports, and also to open up to his father and find ways to interact and engage with him. The joy I felt for Tyler and his dad, for our family, words cannot express.

What the doctors and professionals thought was a daunting forecast for my son's life living with autism, turned out to be more like uncovering a buried treasure. I found out that Tyler had a sense of humor. I'm not even sure what made me notice. One of the hallmarks of autism spectrum disorder is difficulty grasping abstract concepts or emotionally connecting with others. What a pleasant surprise it was to know that he understood what made something funny and could make others laugh as well. Eye opening is an understatement. Time and again, Tyler defied the odds. But when I think about it, his father and I are so comical that he was either destined to laugh or not have sense enough to cry.

And then Tyler wanted to learn to ride a bike. *Have mercy.* He had been amazing at everything else he had put his mind and hands to. So, why was I nervous? I realized it was outside of my skill set. Not because I didn't know how to ride a bike, albeit according to my mom, I had training wheels on my bike until I was about thirteen. My own fear of falling and the idea that my autistic son might fail, or worse than that, could be described as overboard. I couldn't stand the thought that Tyler might hurt himself. Strangely and wonderfully enough, this was about the time when his father's dad skills kicked in big time.

I was concerned that he wanted to teach him to ride a bike so early. Tyler was about seven or eight, and that seemed early to me for a child with autism. Many kids with autism have issues with hand-eye coordination and sending signals to the brain that the body must execute.

Tyler was fascinated by wheels and things that spun, so he'd go sit on the curb in our cul-de-sac for hours watching the kids ride their bikes in the circle. Occasionally, he would run after them and try to stick his hand in the spokes as they rode them. I was terrified he would be run down, or his fingers be cut off.

Much to my chagrin, his dad came home with a blue stingray bike with mountain wheels and said, "I'm going to teach him to ride this weekend." My first reaction was this *fool* has lost his damn mind. I gave him the side eye and hoped Tyler wouldn't show much interest, however that was *not* the case.

Early on a sunny, Saturday morning, Tyler's father got him dressed and said, "We're leaving. See you later."

Thoughts kept running through my mind. *Didn't his father understand the danger of teaching Tyler how to ride a bike? Why did this child have to learn to ride a bike now? Wasn't there another skill that he could teach Tyler without the risk of him hurting himself?* Once the questions wore out in my head, I realized that there wasn't any noise coming from outside. No disruptions. No falls. As I cleaned the house, I peeked out the window, and there was no Tyler or his father. At that time, we didn't have cell phones readily available, so I wasn't sure what had taken place. I prayed that his father used better judgement than to have taken my baby out of the cul-de-sac. I had a sneaky suspicion that he'd taken Tyler from our home in Bolingbrook to 35th and Giles where his mom lived to teach him to ride a bike. *He couldn't be that crazy, could he?*

Minutes turned in to hours, three to four to be more exact. When they finally arrived home, Tyler was asleep in the car. His father took him upstairs, returned downstairs and explained that Tyler had done great. He'd taken him to an empty church parking lot, and he had fallen, but only a few times. He needed to make sure that he helped boost him as he got onto the pedals. His father was confident that within a couple of days he'd be able to ride the bike. Even through my worry, I was encouraged and optimistic.

During those days I was exhausted and planning for the next work week. My husband, I recall, frequently needed to make a "run". I knew what that meant—he wouldn't be home for hours and not sure what personality might appear when he did.

Tyler woke up playing. I was in my office in the front of the house. I heard the garage door open, assuming it was Tyler's father, however, he never came into the house. For whatever reason, I never considered that it could've been anyone else, but my husband.

Then laughter echoed from outside. I went to Tyler's room but, he wasn't there. I quickly moved to the backyard, but he wasn't there either. My heart started pounding as I searched the interior of our home, deducing that he had somehow slipped passed me. Though our home was large, there weren't too many places Tyler could've been. Remembering that I heard the garage door open, I stepped into the space, noticing that Randy's car wasn't there. I walked out and into the driveway, and there Tyler was riding around the cul-de-sac like Lance Armstrong just laughing. No hands at times, other moments feet up as if he had been riding for years. He came spinning past me and said, "Look at me!" One of the few times he spoke, and it was with purpose.

I clapped for my baby and said, "Go Tyler-Go Tyler". Fueled with accomplishment I saw that there was so much more in my son than I had ever realized.

How did we get from that scary diagnosis to this young man abounding with personality and unique traits? Trust me, the path was never a straight line. Every day presented new challenges, but also came with many triumphs. Every day begged for plenty of prayers, patience, and persistence.

*"You never step in the same river twice."*

This is one of my favorite sayings. The statement means that since the water is always flowing so rapidly, the river is constantly changing. Well, life with a child with autism is much the same way. No two days are going to be the same, which means being prepared for everything to work or for nothing to work on any given occasion. That doesn't mean giving up or shutting down is an option, it requires that one keeps working to embrace your child and their unique qualities. Research and join communities where parents with children who live with autism are meeting. Try everything you can to develop the connection with your child and people who can help.

If by some unfortunate chance there isn't a community or group available for support, the unwanted solitude can take your mind to a place of fear, wondering, and doubt. At this time, find books to read. Reading will help you to gain knowledge on autism, how to make meaningful connections with your child, and give you the advantages of the resources that are available to you and your family.

# *Chapter 7*

## SARA, TYLER'S GODMOTHER AND MY SISTER-FRIEND

Sara is his godmother, my sorority sister, my friend. My muse and voice of reason when I couldn't rationalize this diagnosis, and often, my child. In an odd way, we had become dependent on each other as we both suffered from the pains of being in marriages that simply weren't meant to be. Yet, she always had the ability to go back to the facts and nothing but the facts. I was a little jealous as I had the occasion to wash down entire packages of Oreo cookies with a vodka chaser in order to manage my feelings. *Where does her pain go?*

Sara always told me when speaking with parents, start with the facts; it was what she practiced.

"According the 2020 the Centers for Disease Control and Prevention (CDC) released new data on the prevalence of autism in the United States.," I stated plainly. "Boys are 4.3 times more likely to be diagnosed on the spectrum."

Tyler was and is her godson. He has autism spectrum disorder.

However, in order to fully understand their relationship, the depth of her love, and the immense appreciation she has for him, you must have insight into the inception, development, and composition of her relationship with me, whom she often fondly refers to as M's.

Our relationship was born out of an encounter that I take great pleasure detailing and describing. To know me is to know my humor and my ability to tell a story. My Mother is a Delta of the Divine Nine, so it was clear, I had to follow the family legacy, no exception nor deviation. So, when I arrived on campus the undergraduate pledgees seemed a bit distant to me, but what did I know? I was a black girl who grew up in a small town in Iowa called Urbandale. The only black girl in the public school system from age 4-17, 1st-12th grade. She and I often laugh about her first thoughts of me.

"Who, I ask you, approaches a pledge of Delta Sigma Theta Sorority Inc. during Hell Week, while navigating the Quad at Bradley University with such laser focus and determination to handle her business? I mean who does that?"

ME, that's who! When I have questions, I want answers, and pursue anyone who may be able to provide me with what I'm looking for. This has served me well over time. Despite what I described as her less-than-enthusiastic response, I eventually pledged the organization, making us sisters on another level. As the story goes, we have shared as girlfriends, sorority sisters and following graduation from Bradley University, we did what most college graduates do, pressed onward to conquer the world and become self-sustainable.

While facing several bumps and bruises along the way, we accomplished a great deal. She enrolled in graduate school at Bradley, graduated, and became a speech-language pathologist and I entered corporate America. In my opinion, her career choice and the skill set she developed could be viewed as both a blessing and a curse as it related to the observation and discovery period leading up to and through the process of Tyler's diagnosis.

During the post-Bradley University era, we remained connected, sharing in life's transitions. Marriage, pregnancy, job changes, child rearing, and divorce, we went through it together. According to her, I possessed awesome organizational skills and social tenacity, single-handedly slaying the role of her wedding coordinator. That was one of the highlights of my life. I ran a tight ship, keeping everyone and everything in line. I used humor and cutting-edge sarcasm to effortlessly make her day that much more special. These same traits would resurface throughout my life's seasons, and they were especially helpful as a coping and self-care strategy.

Following the birth of her second child, she asked me to be the godmother to her daughter, Taylor, and I proudly accepted. To this day, it's one of the greatest honors that I've ever received. A year passed and following the birth of Tyler, I returned the honor, and she became his godmother. The titles and the roles stuck like two-sided tape as both Tyler and Taylor still refer to and address each of us as 'Godmama'.

Over the years, we've shared countless laughs, tears, fears, joys, and concerns. One of many things that remained constant was our faith and the mutual love for our children. Oftentimes, our conversations would start and or end with, "Girl, just pray for me." Even if those words came packaged with laughter, neither of us took that request lightly. Our families sustained each other, and at least monthly if not more, we were over for weekend, holiday, and special occasion visits. Our children looked forward to the visits nearly as much as we did. It was a mini vacation. The trips frequently took all day or lasted late into the evening or overnight. There was so much packed into those excursions; male bonding for our husbands, music, food, laughter, time to play with and get to know Tyler. We escaped from the typical routines of life and its stressors and took the time to just chill. More importantly, as I reflect, it was an incredibly needed time for me. Sara was unaware that I was dealing with a husband who had multiple addictions, and it was taking a toll on me. She was there for the mom, sister-girlfriend connection in all its glory. We laughed at our private jokes, and vented, and commiserated about life.

Sara and I were often able to carve out "we'll be right back" jaunts that morphed into mini shopping runs and inevitably included a stop at Portillo's, a restaurant that became a staple in Tyler's food diet.

It was during one of our family visits, she expressed what seemed to be a passing thought.

"Tyler is really quiet." As a speech-language pathologist, she was intuitively aware of developmental norms and periods of typical and atypical growth. Tyler should've been experiencing a season of flourishing sounds and single-word beginnings.

However, it was the absence of sounds in general that gave her some pause. It was sometime shortly after that thought, during a birthday party for her oldest son, Matthew that things became... well, let's just say it was a celebration and a revelation.

The very advice she had given to parents over the years was now a conversation she labored to have with me, her dear friend, one she must have.

*Chapter 8*

## BEING TYLER'S GODMAMA

"Marietta, autism spectrum disorder is a neurodevelopmental disorder characterized by challenges with social skills, repetitive and restrictive behaviors, verbal and nonverbal communication, as well as by unique strengths and differences," Sara explained or reminded me on numerous occasions. "Autism doesn't discriminate on the basis of ethnicity, race, religion, gender, socioeconomic level, or geographic region." As much as I appreciated the scientific data, I struggled with the sterile perspective. I know she loved me, and she loved Tyler, yet her inability to take off her clinical hat became a source of frustration to me over time.

When Tyler and I arrived, for the party following a reasonably long car-ride from home, many of the party guests had already arrived. It was a relatively small gathering with immediate family and a few friends. Nothing out of the norm, however after the typical exchange of hugs and verbal greetings, Tyler became increasingly upset, or as she called it "dysregulated." He screamed and cried uncontrollably. I don't recall any one person overreacting to this behavior, but I remember *my* feelings inside. A mixture of panic, discomfort, and embarrassment. Just as I felt my eyebrows draw into the middle of my forehead, my heartbeat took on a chaotic beat. I quickly scooped him up in my arms while simultaneously muttering something to the effect of "We need to go upstairs."

After ascending the stairs in what I thought were in leaps and bounds, Tyler and I disappeared into a bedroom and closed the door. The actual sequence of events that followed is a bit of a blur, but I do remember attempting once more to join the party before announcing that we needed to leave. I checked in with Sara later that night and talked about Tyler's reaction. That opened the door to a conversation about taking Tyler to have a comprehensive developmental evaluation.

She later shared this thought: "As a mother of two, who are now young adults, and after experiencing her own "be woke" moments during the child-rearing years, I believe that as moms we know in our hearts when something is not quite right with our children and when that something requires our special attention. Dealing with it or addressing it is not always something that we are comfortable pursuing or something we can address immediately, and in some cases not at all. It's like God gives moms that keen sense of perception and protective mechanisms that sometimes awakens us in the middle of the night, sometimes keeps us up all night, and sometimes at least for a period of time, immobilizes us. I also have come to believe that if we remain prayerful, trusting, and believing in God, seeking him out for direction and remaining open to his guidance, he will show us what needs to be done. Not only that, but he will lead us to who, where, and how to get it done."

This brings me to one of her favorite scripture verses that I keep close to heart:

*"Now faith is the substance of things hoped for, the evidence of things not seen"* -Hebrews 11:1, KJV.

Following our conversation, I wasted no time in scheduling a date for Tyler's evaluation.

Before Tyler's diagnosis of ASD, she stated that she was blessed not only to be introduced to, but also be involved in an evidenced-based treatment philosophy that for years since has empowered her and other families who have children with speech, language and communication disorders called for Developmental, Individual, Relationship Based Intervention (DIR). The DIR model is a framework that helps clinicians, parents, and educators conduct comprehensive assessments in order to develop educational and/or intervention programs tailored to the unique challenges and strengths of each child. I mention it here because it was both relevant and effective for Tyler. DIR allowed for discussion, exploration and insight into the sensory-based challenges and needs that Tyler exhibited—self-imposed diet restrictions, language and social communication needs and challenges, as well as family care and well-being. Tyler received his comprehensive evaluation, (today it's referred to as a medical diagnostic for children up to three years of age) at the University of Illinois at Chicago's Family Clinic. The team was under the guidance of a well-known and respected developmental pediatrician in the field. The evaluation team members included a social worker, psychologist and speech and language pathologist.

Although Sara was a member of that diagnostic team, she recused herself from Tyler's evaluation for obvious reasons. She was, however, interviewed regarding my observations of Tyler and his development. She remained neutral, emotionally detached, and objective. She had approached the evaluation in a professional speech-language pathologist capacity. However, the emotional overlay was one that she couldn't ignore.

On the day of the evaluation, Tyler, my husband, and I arrived at the clinic. Anxiety had a chokehold on all of us, even Sara. We arrived well prepared with snacks and various accoutrements. According to her, the actual evaluation day was relatively "benign". In other words, it was noneventful. That's how she felt, however that is *not* how I felt.

Following the diagnostic team meeting, the internal clinic meeting where test scores, professional opinions, and recommendations for the next steps were given. Sara was invited in as a member of the team and given the news of Tyler's diagnosis. Later, she expressed the gamut of emotions she experienced with the news—a mixture of sadness, hope, and excitement. Sadness because she understood the rough and lonely course Tyler would have to make; hope because she knew I'd do everything to make sure that my son was successful; and excited at the new prospects for treatment.

Sara attended the feedback session as a family member. We all were anxious about how the diagnosis would be perceived. Research provided us with hope regarding the positive outcomes for early diagnosis and intervention. The next step was to unpack the aforementioned blessing and curse perspective.

As a speech-language pathologist with substantial experience in the field and specific expertise in diagnosis and treatment of children with developmental disabilities, including ASD, Sara had great hopes for Tyler's future. So many times, she sat on the other side of the table, giving the information, listening to the parents' concerns, and trying to help families process the new territory they had to walk, and hopefully move forward. Then she sat, listened, and watched from the perspective of godmother, the person who'll be nurturer and guide for Tyler in the event that my life came to an end.

Having extensive knowledge from a professional standpoint could've been viewed as a curse. Experts rarely offer the bright side of a condition; I imagine as to not get one's hopes up. However, armed with the recommendations from experienced leaders in the field, having a godmama and sister-friend who was a speech-language pathologist well-versed in recently discovered treatments, with an awesome holistic perspective for children who live with autism and their families, Sara felt hopeful and inspired. Information plus faith put us in a good position for Tyler's success.

From an outlook of faith, I believe God strategically places us where we need to be at the precise time needed, equipping us with the exact tools we need. It wasn't too much later that she experienced what felt like the "calm before the storm."

Following the information that was communicated during the family feedback session, the room remained quiet. I'm not sure how long the silence rested in the air, but I couldn't stand it. The tears I fought to hold back fell without regard.

*Breathe, Marietta. Breathe.* I wasn't altogether certain what direction this diagnosis was supposed to take and knew I couldn't do anything while having any level of a meltdown. Sara was there to remind me that I was great mother to Tyler and that we'd be okay. I collected the pieces of my dream and sprang into action, asking questions and taking notes. There wasn't a moment to waste trying to put into motion what needed to be done. I went into super-go mode, taking the recommendations in stride and single-handedly planning right there to get them into play that very afternoon. Organizing schedules, plotting connections, and creating opportunities for success is in my wheelhouse, so I handled that portion, to Sara's surprise. Obtaining the required information, strategizing, and executing the plan was the most normal and comfortable part of my life.

We left the clinic that day, and I spoke with Sara that evening. We discussed options for early intervention, including DIR, and I shared a bit about my husband's reaction during the ride home. We talked periodically over the course of the next several days as we made the plans for Tyler's journey with autism.

One day in particular, I called Sara while she cleaned her house. She told me that she was cleaning a bathroom mirror and we laughed about some event that I can't remember at the point of writing this memoir. However, the discussion took a turn when we got to the recap of a conversation that occurred between me and my husband. My dear friend was ill-prepared for what came next.

I related my struggle and issue, in denial of Tyler's diagnosis. I continued with the inquiry, wanting to know if she was a speech-language pathologist, why she didn't realize what was going on with our son sooner. Later on, Sara described her reaction, what I deemed "her mirror moment"—she froze staring square in the mirror, feeling a bit of the blessing/curse thing, second guessing her professional abilities. Anger, guilt, and embarrassment weighed in her heart. She noticed what was happening with Tyler but wanted to be cautious; no one wants an unasked-for diagnosis even if your friend has degrees and letters behind her name. She loved her godson like he was her own. Maybe she should've said something sooner. Would her observation have saved us any more heartache or confusion? Probably not. That's water under the bridge. I felt awful that I mentioned the conversation.

All in all, Sara was a great resource for DIR and for its incorporation with professional reflective supervision; this was an integral part of a therapist's practice. Reflective supervision is where a client is allowed to ask questions while the therapist helps them to answer their own inquiries. I sought guidance so that I could process the entire experience from both a professional and personal standpoint. From suspicion to diagnosis to planning, it was an exhausting course. During, Sara counseled us on the stages of grieving that terminally ill people experience prior to death or the loss of a loved one. These same stages can and often do occur when a family receives a new diagnosis like autism in a young child. For certain, I grieved for all the dreams and hopes I had for him.

Shock, denial, bargaining, guilt, anger, depression, and acceptance— these are the seven stages of grief. It was during therapy that I was informed that these stages don't necessarily happen in the order listed. Families are unique in the manner and time it takes them to move through each stage. Sara was also informed that she needed to allow herself to grieve as a family member.

Sara did what served me and Tyler well. I have deferred to my faith and remained prayerful. The information and time spent in reflection was humbling, revealing, comforting, made sense, and applicable for this experience and many more since.

The days, months, and years between Tyler's diagnosis and the present have been filled with valleys and mountain top journeys for me and my precious son. So many events happened, inquiries made, advice given, and resources requested. Opinions were offered, laughter was shared, and tears were shed regarding Tyler and his growth, and well as her own.

She often expressed that it was a pleasure to observe me, and how she admires my tenacity, determination, and faith in action. Even if she doesn't agree with me, she's patient with me. Over the years, I periodically thank my dear friend and express my gratitude for being a regular and integral part of Tyler's life. At one time, I thought she was uncomfortable with this expression she is a humble spirit; she never saw what she did as an act of extraordinary sacrifice, and God knows all that she did was beyond the limits of friendship.

As parents, it's important—no crucial—for us to prepare our children when faced with differences to be respectful, be kind, respond in kindness, and to respond with and express empathy. The must learn to treat others the way we want to be treated regardless of our race, ethnicity, socioeconomic class, religion, and or emotional/social and intellectual differences and challenges. We do this being the example of the type of conduct we desire to see in our environment. That led me to ponder the old parenting standby phrase: "Do as I say. Not as I do." I've adapted this phrase to "Do as I do, not just as I say." Modeling latter behavior is second nature to me.

Sara often shared that even her own children have, in their uninformed youthful experiences, been guilty of giggling and perhaps giving awkward stares when encountering an individual with special needs and the manner in which they react or respond to the surrounding atmosphere. However, "to know better is to do better". As a parent, these are optimal teachable moments, prime time if you will, to prepare, and expect growth in our children.

My god daughter, Taylor, would occasionally ask questions about Tyler, like why he ate the same things all the time or why he didn't talk. Sara casually explained and answered questions, sharing nuggets of information in the moments when she observed her daughter's confused facial expressions. Although the world may distinguish between, and some may even discriminate based upon those who are labeled as "atypical" or "neurotypical," she has expressed how blessed she felt that her children enjoyed being in Tyler's company. To them, he was family. They've always had a genuine love for him.

Fast forward to the present, Tyler has grown and developed into a respectful, courteous, handsome young man with a work ethic to be reckoned with. He's a product of parents with great faith who sacrificed, became informed, and advocated for him. My journey as a mother of a child diagnosed with ASD, Sara is the first to tell anybody how dedicated and knowledgeable I am about autism spectrum disorder. After all, she watched this part of my life unfold from its inception. She never expected anything less, as I remained driven to be an advocate and provide the best educational, social, and personal experiences possible, not only for Tyler, but also for other families; I was a testament that the parents of children with autism can be successful. She says I'm like the energizer bunny—I just keep going and giving.

Recently, I paid the blessings forward, by immersing myself into a number of endeavors, sharing some of my time, talents, and resources within Sara's community of faith and working with the children who had special needs.

One could read this and think how blessed Tyler and I really are. The truth is we've always been.

"Faith by itself, if it has no works, is dead." (James 2:17 NRSV)

Tyler is where both faith and works together excelled.

# Chapter 9

## BEING TYLER'S NANA

Sometimes all you have is Mama. I mean *really* the one who bore you, the one that knows you better than yourself. How can she see a way out of no way?

My mother first got to meet her grandbaby at my home. This is her account—

What I saw was a beautiful, baby boy with big, beautiful eyes, long eyelashes, and a head full of black curls. I was so proud my youngest daughter had become a mother with this adorable little baby boy. I lived in Iowa, and I wanted him to know his Nana and Paw Paw even though we were three hundred thirty-three miles away. I spent a lot of time driving back and forth to Chicago so he would get to know me and remember my voice. We developed a beautiful bond. I'd sing to him in the rocking chair in his bedroom. I couldn't carry a tune, but I managed to sing "Rock a Bye Baby". He seemed to recognize me from my singing to him, it was always the same song. If he was a little restless and crying, I'd take him to the rocking chair and sing. That always did the trick. His mother would say he thinks you are his mother.

He was diagnosed at around 2 years of age. I didn't know what to expect. I was at an event in Des Moines, and I shared the news with my friend, Sally. We were in the same Breakfast Club, and she told us about her son who was autistic. I hadn't previously paid a lot of attention to the minute details she shared with us about Ronnie. Two days later, I received a book in the mail titled "Autism Speaks" as a gift from Sally. I read the book from front to back and still didn't know how this diagnosis would affect my Tyler. I knew it was time to talk to God and have him help me understand what I was reading. I wondered what could be done for him. I couldn't comprehend what my daughter was going through. She took this diagnosis head on, determined to learn everything about this disorder. She was relentless in her need to know everything possible and what could be done to help her first born child. She wouldn't accept negative comments or any form of discouraging remarks. I know God was with her every step of the journey, which I could tell was challenging and exhaustive. As far as I could tell, the thought of giving up never entered her mind.

When she met with these professionals, I had the privilege of being with her at some of her appointments. The psychologist, developmental pediatrician, speech and language pathologist, and the learning consultant were some of the professionals we met with. They seemed taken aback with what she knew about autism as well as their professions. Lord, I don't know how she stayed so focused.

I sat quietly admiring my daughter and how this mother didn't give up and she wouldn't allow the team she was working with to do so. I often told her Tyler was a gift from God and that God gives special kids to special parents. As a matter of fact, I gave her a beautiful poem about special kids and special parents which I had framed and it's still hanging up on her office wall. I read books where some autistic children didn't make eye contact, Tyler always made eye contact as he got older. He would smile and laugh and loved to be hugged.

On a lighter subject, Tyler has had a computer since he was two years old. He had his tapes he enjoyed listening to and played them by himself. I remember my daughter telling me Tyler was walking around the house saying things she didn't understand, she said it sounded like Spanish, but she doubted it. So, she looked at his tapes and he had put one on Spanish and had learned to speak the Spanish that was on the tape. We laughed about that. I told her I need him to teach me Spanish.

There are so many humorous and loving things I remember about when Tyler was visiting me. I was so grateful that his mother was always happy to let Tyler go to Iowa with his Nana to spend several days. He loved to ride in my car because I had all of his favorite songs: Barney, Elmo, Big Bird, etc., on tape. We smiled and laughed, singing those songs all the way home.

One day, I decided to take him to the petting zoo, not knowing how he would react, so I held him close to me. Well, when he saw the goats standing there, he took off running to them to rub them, taking a good look at their faces. Boy, what a pleasant surprise! He wasn't afraid of any of the animals, so we spent lots of time petting the other ones. He became a pro at petting them. It was so funny to see some of the other kids afraid of the animals, but not my Tyler.

On another visit, my sister rode with me to pick him up, and I informed her to not take his hand, let him come to you first. No big deal for him, he took her hand as we left to go to my car. Tyler never cried when he left his mother. We always stopped halfway to Des Moines to give him a break from sitting so long and to get something to eat. We had to make sure not to look at him until I got him situated with the booster chair and put his food on the tray. We would talk and eat and eventually he would start to eat. He loved chicken tenders, fries, and orange juice. Tyler has always been a good eater.

When they moved to West Bloomfield, Michigan, he was a lot older. Sometimes, when I took him to school, he was so proud to introduce his teacher to his Nana. Tyler has always had a photographic memory, once he goes somewhere, he remembers and can go back there with no problem. Well, this particular day Tyler and I wanted to go to Burger

King for lunch, so I asked him if he knew where there was a Burger King.

"Yes, Nana," he replied and off we went to find this Burger King. We rode for about forty-five minutes, and I became a little doubtful, but we kept going until we finally arrived, and it was closed for remodeling. We found another place to eat on the way back. When I told his mother, she said "Oh my goodness, you were in Ann Arbor, Michigan." Tyler's memory worked so well that he had recalled a Burger King he saw once miles from home. Well, that was just Tyler coming through again.

As time moved on, Tyler entered high school. He did very well in high school. I asked him if he had a girlfriend and he told me, "Not really". I didn't pursue that topic any further as boys can be shy on the subject. Tyler was a great athlete, and popular, he was also a computer geek.

I went to his high school graduation and was so proud of his accomplishments. I thanked God for his progress. He was so proud at his graduation ceremonies, especially when they called his name as he walked across the stage. He spotted us when he entered the auditorium. I waved a white scarf so he would know where we were sitting.

After the ceremony, his teachers spoke so highly of my guy. Each spoke of how he carried himself, worked hard to get good grades, and respected his teachers. Oh, by the way, Tyler graduated with honors. Not bad for someone who the first doctors weren't sure was ever going to speak. Those are wonderful memories that will always be with me. His mother had a big, beautiful buffet of delicious food for Tyler, his friends, and their parents and out of town-guests.

I once read this article on how to prepare a child with a neurological condition for life on their own, whether they are going off to college, getting a job and/or their first apartment. My daughter had started preparing Tyler for his next step in life long before that time came. Tyler knew how to wash and fold his clothes and hang them up. He knew how to fix his own breakfast, lunch, and dinner. He kept his room clean and in order at all times. He knew how to clean his bathroom. He has always been very particular about where he put his things. His closet had all of his clothes hung up; short sleeves, long sleeves, jackets, and sweaters a certain way and all hung up. I told him to come home with me and tidy up my closets. He also worked a part-time office job during the summer.

Tyler attended Clemson University, Clemson LIFE, College of Education Program. He finished all of his classes again with honors. He even took classes from the regular program like calculus, which he did very well in.

I saw my grandson go from a teenager to a man. Emotions poured at the graduation ceremony when I saw in the program that he was one of the speakers. It all came rushing on me at one time. His mother spent time at countless conferences, parent-teacher sessions, and school events, which wasn't easy while holding a position as the highest-ranking Black woman at Microsoft. He matured and carried himself like a gentleman at all times. It was more than I could keep inside of me; I cried tears of joy. I miss him now that he's grown and on his own, but I know God is taking care of him. I'm so comforted by that.

We took so many pictures that they would have filled a photo gallery. Tyler soaked it all up with a big smile.

My Tyler is living on his own, working a full-time job, has his own apartment with his friends and enjoying life. A very responsible young man. As I look back over the last 20 years, I still get choked up. My daughter, his teachers, counselors, family, and Nana never gave up on Tyler.

I'm reminded of my favorite saying: *Dear Lord, thank you for holding me and my family close to your heart this day and always.*

# Chapter 10

## TYLER THE COLLEGE GRADUATE AND BEYOND

There is a moment when you know one chapter will end as a new one begins. I'd lost my sister to sepsis and my marriage was more than over. The trauma from these events made it difficult to rejoice for Tyler and all of his accomplishments, and he deserved to be celebrated. How was I supposed to muster up the courage to leave all the years of addiction, emotional neglect, and dysfunction that had destroyed me? Jumping off the Poseidon was the only way. For a quick history reference, the USS Poseidon was a Royal Navy Parthian-class submarine. It launched in 1929 and sunk in 1931. The part of life wasn't about hopping from the frying pan into the fire; it was about leaving a plummeting vessel and swimming to the surface for air.

In an effort to think through the planning for the future, it was very important to me to have someone to look out for Tyler. As the younger sister of a special needs sibling, I always had her back. I wanted the same for Tyler.

In 1998, my second son, Connor, was born prematurely. He weighed 2 pounds with a variety of issues, made far worse by a urinary tract infection. This ultimately impacted his hearing, and he was diagnosed over time with a learning disability and auditory neuropathy, a rare type of hearing loss caused by the disruption of nerve impulses traveling from the inner ear to the brain. Its cause is unknown, and as of the time of this writing, there is no cure. I know other parents in those circumstances would've torn their clothes, devastated by grief, guilt, and denial, angry with doctors for not having better answers. Life with Tyler allowed me to know better and to do better. I simply prayed and asked God to save my little boy, no matter what his challenges. I'd always be there. I thank God daily that he spared my son, in spite of his various challenges. Tyler is a great big brother as he always supported him and made sure he was safe. We never know what is in front of us or *why* it's in front of us, we only know that we have to roll with the punches. At some point, I'll most likely spend time writing a book about Connor and the challenges he faced, and the discrimination the deaf community encounters. Suffice to say, I have picked up the mantle to help him based upon my oldest son.

*"He leaves the 99 to go after that one sheep." Luke 15 :4-7*

When I witnessed throughout the years of my friends' children growing up and going away to the colleges and post-secondary education, I always kept that grain of hope. Maybe one day Tyler could have a similar experience. I privately saved money in a college fund regardless of how foolish it might have seemed to others. I still had dreams for *my* son. Each milestone he passed in school, each sporting activity he mastered, made the vision for him so much clearer. All things that "typical" children and young adults experienced, Tyler did, too. His father taught him to be athletic; how to ride a bike, how to dunk a basketball, and how to master their favorite Xbox Games. Tyler was gifted in basketball, baseball, and swimming. His father deserves a great deal of credit for being an outstanding coach. However, my position at Microsoft made honing those gaming skills a whole lot easier.

Tyler was an excellent student and mastered so many things seemed impossible when I think back to the day that he was diagnosed. His sense of humor, asking questions about girls, going to the Prom, being a hit at the high school sock hop because he is an excellent dancer were all things that allowed me to keep a glimmer of hope.

Tyler attended Centennial High School in Alpharetta Georgia, where upon stepping foot on campus had deemed himself the Fresh Prince of Bel Air, one of his favorite television characters. He was affectionately referred to as "FP". My son is a handsome and polite young man with swagger who happens to live with autism—one could only appreciate this if you are the parent of an autistic child or have done extended research about the condition. Understanding this disorder manifests in so many ways, from mild to severe, I know how Tyler developed, even with all of the work educators, doctors, and his parents put in, was not short of miraculous.

Over the years, my husband poured his love of basketball into Tyler. He was a very accomplished basketball player at Kenwood Academy in Hyde Park so to have a son who stood 6'2" in high school was a dream come true. Their Saturday mornings were consumed with time at the gym or the neighborhood playground close to where he was raised to shoot hoops. By then, one of his addictions was in remission and his focus on Tyler amplified. He would often tell Tyler just how good he was at basketball. Given what I had read about kids with autism, Tyler wasn't supposed to have a grasp on hand-eye coordination, but his father made sure his son not only learned that skill, but also mastered it. I wondered if he was just trying to relive his glory days and unable to really assess Tyler's ability. Nonetheless, Tyler and his friend Erik were legends in the special needs world at Centennial, especially on the basketball squad. They were the tallest and only two Black players. And no bias, they were the two best looking on the team as well.

One day, I went to one of his playoff games. I was often busy at my job, but he and his father wanted me to attend so I carved out some time to go. His father focused on his athletic skills, while my attention weighed on his academic repertoire. I feel the combination of his parents assistance and persistence, made Tyler a shining example of what can happen with love and faith.

I arrived at the basketball stadium, and the team was warming up in the uniforms I had washed and prepared so many times before. Immediately, I began "fan-momming", waving and screaming "Go, Tyler."

The game kicked off and I was impressed by the fact these special needs boys were getting it— they could HOOP! The exchange was remarkable, and it was a serious game. I was especially shocked at just how good Erik was and how he and Tyler fist-bumped each other, carrying on like NBA ballplayers. Chills ran through my body like a jolt of electricity—*this must be what parents of typical kids feel*. I'm not sure if it was the first half or the second, but this happened: while on the opposing team's basket, Erik broke the opponent's pass. Tyler was already positioned down court. Erik threw him the ball, all the team members headed to the opposite end of the floor and Tyler, my autistic son slam dunked the damn ball. I almost crapped myself.

His dad went nuts. "I *told* you he could dunk!"

The crowd went wild. Tyler and Erik celebrated like NBA stars dancing, doing hand gyrations and the like.

Tyler ran down the court looked at me, winked, and pointed his finger. It was that moment I exhaled; I knew my son would be alright. Different, but all right! I cried that night knowing everything I had been through all the pain I had felt was worth it.

As he approached the completion of his high school years, it was evident to the teachers and to me that he wouldn't "age out". Aging out is part of the Individuals with Disabilities Education Act (IDEA) which lays out the educational guidelines for children and young adults by state law under which the school district is no longer responsible for education and support after a certain age. I was thankful that this wasn't the case for Tyler, but still frightened for what the future had in store for him.

One event, one milestone, one success, one failure—all of these steps could only be taken one at a time. This time around I needed to think about what would be next. He had done so well in work study programs at companies like Siemens and other corporations that began inclusion programs in the workplace, supporting individuals with unique needs. I was as proud as any parent could be when his counselor said, "Tyler can do whatever he wants. Every work study setting we place him in, he succeeds."

Under the guidance and help of the amazing team at Centennial High School in Alpharetta, Georgia, we began to formulate a plan. We had moved four times to new cities as I pursued my executive career at Microsoft. Before each move, I did the proper research on which states offered the best programs for individuals with special needs, starting with my state's local autism society.

After a great deal of research, I'd choose the new location. Once I arrived, I selected the best school district that had advanced programs for special needs students. For us, they were programs that were inclusive so he could grow alongside his peers. Each child is different, and it's up to you to do the research and find what will be a good fit for your child and family.

As the plan hatched, programs popped up in a few universities around the country that supported "high functioning" students, providing a collegiate experience that included education and extended preparedness for independent living. After much reviewing, we chose the institution that was the most progressive campus life experience built on a similar 4-year college where face-to-face visits and tours for acceptance were required: Clemson University. The ClemsonLIFE™ program a collegiate experience that prepares young men and women with intellectual disabilities for competitive employment and independent living through a combination of academic coursework and career exploration. The program is designed for students who desire a post-secondary lifestyle on a college campus. The program incorporates functional academics, independent living, employment, and social/leisure skills in a public university setting with the goal of producing self-sufficient young adults.

At the time of publication, there are similar programs at many private and public universities. I could write another book on his college days, and a lot of it would be about Clemson Tiger football. The program entered its current golden age while Tyler was in school there and he had season tickets, enjoyed every home game, and picked up some amazing life skills along the way. He lived in a dorm apartment with three other guys, walked to campus or rode his bike to classes, and participated in a majority of the university's social activities.

I distinctly remember his Godmother and his Nana accompanying his father and I to his graduation ceremony. As we moved around the campus with him, it was astonishing how many students knew him, said how amazing he was, and recalled fond memories of being with him in class. It was a far departure from the early years before inclusion was commonplace.

"Wow," my mom said. "I think Tyler is a big man on campus, literally!"

There are a few milestone moments in his life that really resonated. When he graduated from high school, when we dropped him off for college, when he called after the first Clemson football championship, and when he was on campus with all the other students enjoying himself. When Deshaun Watson, Clemson's starting quarterback who led the Tigers to the 2016 championship and now plays in the NFL, approached him as he was unpacking his dorm room to catch up with him on what had been happening over the summer. When he shared that he was singing in the church choir and continuing his Bible studies and faith while in college. And that special day when he graduated from college and delivered his acceptance/thank you speech to an auditorium full of people. The little boy who didn't speak until was beyond five was delivering his commencement thank you. He walked with all the other university graduates in 2017 at the all-campus ceremony.

# Chapter 11

## PROUD MAMAS

Sara and I were present and proud moms as we experienced Taylor's college graduation from Hampton in 2016, and Tyler's in 2017. They both have their first "real jobs" and are coincidentally both living miles away from their parental homes. Nothing atypical about the mutual love and admiration they have for each other, or their trajectories into adulthood. During Tyler's graduation celebration, she sat in on a presentation in which he verbally formulated the details of his four year-experience. Her eyes filled with tears of joy, recalling the child that was "so very quiet" and did not speak until almost five years old. In those moments and during the following day's ceremonies and celebrations she recalled how her one-way "Godmama" initiated conversations that were met with brief one-word responses, blossomed into Tyler-initiated calls, texts, and reciprocal conversations with a flurry of multiple conversational turns, expressions of humor and most lovingly, the thing that melts her heart and gives us all such joy. At the end of every conversation, she hears the Tyler-initiated, "I love you, Godmama."

She said, "I pause and respond, "I love you too, Tyler."

*Chapter 12*

## TYLER'S BRIGHT FUTURE

I recall preparing for Tyler's graduation; the date, the people I *knew* would show up, the ones that had always been there and always would be there. I fretted over what I would wear and how I would feel. What made this doubly interesting is that I had requested a separation from his father by this time. See, whether in the back of my mind or in the front, I knew his graduation was my Iyanla moment— *"your work here is done"*. All the years of emotional abuse, torment, ridicule belittlement over my success and failures would finally be over. As we walked across that stage, I would walk into the sunset of this chapter of my life not really knowing what was in front of me. Whatever it was, I knew it would be done and I could be free of the traumatic years of this union. I had another son with special needs to consider that required more, and he would be less apt to understand the family unit being upset. I had done my swan song, retired from Microsoft, traveled more in nine months than a politician and spent more money on shoes and handbags than Imelda Marcos. I deserved to take that bow.

My mother and his godmother flew in, full of excitement and glee. This momentous occasion was the culminations of our labor of love. All of the energy and emotion balled up into one.

When Sara arrived, we hugged and cried for what felt like an eternity. We hadn't seen each other for a while, and our embrace said so much more. It was the unspoken triumph we both felt. All the suggestions she had given me, all of the picture exchange cards she created for me after a long workday, coupled with the disturbances going on in her life. All the phone calls where I burst into tears, her soft-spoken encouragement when she said, "M, we can do this. Hold on. Keep holding onto God's hand and my hand, we got you." I will *never* be able to encapsulate what her strength meant to me.

The minute my mom arrived, and we looked into each other's eyes— no words or tears could express our journey. A mother's love that watched her daughter endure the unimaginable, the unspeakable, in her marriage, and often in her job, yet still found strength to be the very best mother I could be in so many dark places. When we hit the road the next morning to Clemson, it was clear "we did the damn thing".

His father drove as we all relaxed. We were familiar with the campus and where Tyler resided. He had already alerted us to come to Tilman Hall for his pre-graduation presentation on his next steps in life. Walking the campus, this time was nostalgic as I recalled how emotional I was to be able to experience what every other parent felt as they dropped their child off to school. I was blessed to have 4 years to look back upon. The National Championship in Tampa in 2017 we witnessed and a run that seems to this day to never stop of athletic achievement. His friendship with Dabo Sweeney and Deshaun Watson as they were committed to inclusiveness, a feeling like none other.

Entering into Tilman Hall, Tyler met us in shorts and flip flops, looking confident and relaxed, possessing the Senior year swagger.

"What up," he said as he hugged us. I must've held him as long as the day when we dropped him off, maybe 20 minutes. This was the first time I had seen Tyler actually do a presentation with PowerPoint and run the slides. He nailed it and was clear on his career choice. *My baby.* I didn't think I could be more proud of him until the next day when he delivered his commencement speech for his college. I realized that this is what dreams are made of. His nana cried as did his father. I, on the other hand, had no tears. Just swagger as I cheered him on. "You go, T Money! You go, boyfriend."

It was and is the finest hour of my life, his birth would be second, of course. I came back a week later to witness him graduating in the big stadium, and it was the most beautiful experience for him. Classmates roared in Little John Coliseum as his name was called. Tyler had the honor of shaking the hand of the President of Clemson University, John Clements. He came dressed to kill. It was the finale of a lifetime, and it couldn't have been any better.

Tyler is now an active member of the Clemson/Greenville Community, with an amazing occupation and a future like one only I could imagine for him.

My journey continues. This is my story— a story of hope, belief, and perseverance that I hope will inspire other mothers never to give up. As with any happy ending, life wouldn't be life without at least one twist, right? I can honestly say that all of the curveballs that came our way made life a lot more interesting and in a lot of great ways.

*"The Lord is close to the brokenhearted, he rescues those whose spirits are crushed."* -Psalms 34:18.

Remember what I wrote at the beginning about faith, hope, and love? If you are still here at the end of reading this book, I'd guess that you are either the parent, relative, or friend of a special needs child. They are truly beautiful, aren't they? Sometimes their lives can be painful and challenging, but isn't it the same with all children? Doesn't that make the genuine smiles, the laughter, and the hugs and 'I love yous' all the more sweet when they come? If you *are* a parent who has observed the differences or have received the news that your child has been diagnosed with ASD or any other condition that is going to have a profound effect on their lives, I encourage you to take the bull by the horns and start learning everything you can. Ask every question you can think of. Advocate for your child with the passion and purpose that God created you for. You'll never know just how amazing you can be until there's someone counting on you to help them get through this crazy world, but don't try and do it alone. Surround yourself with people who believe in you and can support you along the way because there are going to be times when you need a hand to hold, or a shoulder to cry on. They'll have arms to wrap around you and give the reassurance that you are doing the right things.

In short, you and your support system need to be filled with hope, love, and faith to get there. The journey might be long, but the things you experience along the way, and that beautiful vision of your child becoming who they were meant to be is worth every step you take.

We never know what life has in store for us. That is left up to God. Have faith and fight for your child.

*"Jesus looked at them and said, "With man this is impossible, but with God all things are possible"*. -Mathew 19:26

# About the Author

Marietta Colston-Davis a mother, a professional, inspirational leader, and a believer in the impossible! She is a seasoned sales professional with an extensive career in the technology industry. She has held critical positions at IBM, Lotus Development, Ameritech, Tata Consulting and most recently the role of vice president of U.S. Dynamics at Microsoft Corporation. Marietta was responsible for leading more than 400 sales, marketing and technical experts serving Microsoft's business customers with Dynamics ERP and CRM Solutions. While at Microsoft, Marietta successfully managed and grew multiple business at Microsoft to $1B and triple digit growth milestones. Her diverse portfolio extends to mentoring strong leaders into key roles, acting in an advisory capacity to incubation and small startups. She currently sits on the National Board of Youth Villages, a private nonprofit organization dedicated to helping emotionally and behaviorally troubled children and their families. The organization assists more than 23,000 children and families each year from more than 20 states and Washington, D.C. A graduate of Bradley University, she also graduated with an MBA from Loyola University, as well as executive advanced leadership classes at Harvard University. She was inducted into the Spelman College "Game Changer" Hall of Fame for her work in 2015 additionally she has been a sought-after speaker at Morehouse College, Georgia Tech as well as Women in Technology

www.mariettasmusings.com

www.ingramcontent.com/pod-product-compliance
Lightning Source LLC
Chambersburg PA
CBHW060254150626
46553CB00019BA/2332